BLAST THROUGH THE PAST!

AN UNDERCOVER HISTORY OF SPIES AND SECRET AGENTS

Rachel Minay

W

Franklin Watts
Published in paperback in Great Britain in 2019 by The Watts Publishing Group

Produced for Franklin Watts by
White-Thomson Publishing Ltd
www.wtpub.co.uk

Credits
Series Editor: Izzi Howell
Series Designer: Rocket Design (East Anglia) Ltd
Series Consultant: Philip Parker

The publisher would like to thank the following for permission to reproduce their pictures: Alamy/Stocktrek Images, Inc. 6r; Wikimedia Commons/vlasta2 6l; Corbis/Leemage 7; Wikimedia Commons/Joseph Martin Kronheim (1810–96) 8; Corbis/Hamid Sardar 9; Shutterstock/ayelet-keshet 10t; Shutterstock/Radu Razvan 10br; Shutterstock/wdeon 10bl; Wikimedia Commons/Shadowleafcutlery 11l; Shutterstock/Jamen Percy 11r; istock/duncan1890 12; Alamy/World History Archive 13t; Alamy/Lebrecht Music and Arts Photo Library 13b; Shutterstock/Lightspring 14l; Shutterstock/Everett Historical 14r; Wikimedia Commons/The Central Intelligence Agency 15; Library of Congress/Lindsley, H. B. 16; Library of Congress 17t; Topfoto/The Granger Collection 17c; Corbis/AS400 DB 17b; Shutterstock/Everett Historical 18; Shutterstock/Steve Mann 19t; Shutterstock/Neftali 19c; Alamy/AF archive 19b; Alamy/AJD images 20; Alamy/INTERFOTO 21t; Library of Congress/Bain News Service 21c; Library of Congress 21b; Shutterstock/Everett Historical 22, 22–23; Shutterstock/Sue Stokes 23; Snap Stills/REX Shutterstock 24; Alamy/Ian Shaw 25; Shutterstock/BorisVetshev 26t; Corbis/Bettmann 26b; Library of Congress/Higgins, Roger 27l; Shutterstock/Everett Historical 27r; Shutterstock/Rena Schild 29t; Shutterstock/Ollyy 29b; Stefan Chabluk 31. All design elements from Shutterstock.

Every attempt has been made to clear copyright. Should there be any inadvertent omission please apply to the publisher for rectification.

ISBN 978 1 4451 4934 9

Printed in China

Franklin Watts
An imprint of
Hachette Children's Group
Part of The Watts Publishing Group
Carmelite House
50 Victoria Embankment
London EC4Y 0DZ

An Hachette UK Company
www.hachette.co.uk

www.franklinwatts.co.uk

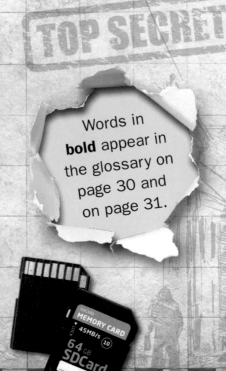

Words in **bold** appear in the glossary on page 30 and on page 31.

CONTENTS

SPIES AND SECRET AGENTS
THROUGH HISTORY

A spy is someone who collects secret information from an enemy or rival organisation. A secret agent is a spy who gathers information for a country. People have used spies throughout history to gain an advantage over others – this might mean a government finding out what kind of weapons the enemy has or a company stealing information about a competitor's product.

What it was like to be a spy and live your life in the shadows? How did the lives of these undercover agents change over time?

This timeline shows you the names, nationalities and dates of the people mentioned in this book.

Described ancient spies in his book The Art of War

Sun Tzu (China) ●
c. 500 BCE

Julius Caesar (Rome) ●
100–44 BCE

NORTH AMERICA

ATLANTIC OCEAN

SOUTH AMERICA

The only Cold-War spies executed in the USA

Led the team that cracked the Enigma code

Spied for Germany in both World Wars

Edward Snowden (USA) 1983~

Julius and Ethel Rosenberg (USA) 1918/1915–1953

Kim Philby (Britain) 1912–1988

Alan Turing (Britain) 1912–1954

Klaus Fuchs (Germany/Britain) 1911–1988

Lawrence of Arabia (Britain) 1888–1935

Fritz Duquesne (South Africa) 1877–1956

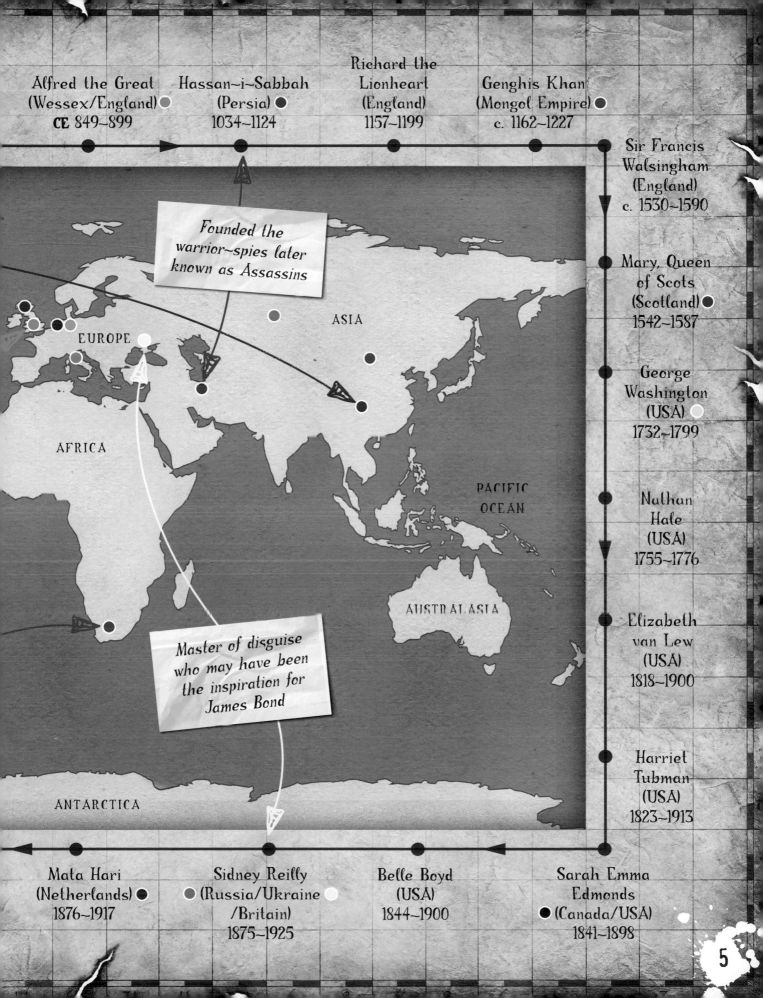

Alfred the Great
(Wessex/England)
CE 849–899

Hassan-i-Sabbah
(Persia)
1034–1124

Richard the
Lionheart
(England)
1157–1199

Genghis Khan
(Mongol Empire)
c. 1162–1227

Sir Francis
Walsingham
(England)
c. 1530–1590

Mary, Queen
of Scots
(Scotland)
1542–1587

George
Washington
(USA)
1732–1799

Nathan
Hale
(USA)
1755–1776

Elizabeth
van Lew
(USA)
1818–1900

Harriet
Tubman
(USA)
1823–1913

Founded the
warrior-spies later
known as Assassins

Master of disguise
who may have been
the inspiration for
James Bond

ASIA

EUROPE

AFRICA

PACIFIC
OCEAN

AUSTRALASIA

ANTARCTICA

Mata Hari
(Netherlands)
1876–1917

Sidney Reilly
(Russia/Ukraine
/Britain)
1875–1925

Belle Boyd
(USA)
1844–1900

Sarah Emma
Edmonds
(Canada/USA)
1841–1898

ANCIENT AGENTS

007 BCE...? If you think secret agents like James Bond are a modern invention, think again. As long as there has been warfare, it's been vital to know what your enemy is up to.

Five kinds of spy

Around 500 BCE, ancient China was made up of different states that were often at war. Sun Tzu, a famous military general, believed advantage in war needed five kinds of spy:

1. local spies
2. inward spies (the enemy's officials)
3. converted spies (**double agents**)
4. doomed spies (spies that you use to spread false information before losing them to the enemy)
5. surviving spies (who brought back information from enemy camps).

SUPER SPYMASTER

NAME: Sun Tzu

NATIONALITY: Chinese

AKA: Awesome ancient author

ACHIEVEMENTS:
Sun Tzu wrote about the importance of **espionage** in his influential book *The Art of War.*

HE SAID WHAT?

'If you know the enemy and know yourself, you need not fear the result of a hundred battles'.

Sun Tzu saw spies as essential in order to 'know the enemy'. His brilliant strategies helped to win a lot of battles.

Secret messages

In **ancient Greece**, the different **city-states** used spies against each other or distant enemies, such as **Persia**. The Greeks used lots of tricks to pass on secret messages – one was to shave a spy's head and write a message on it. The spy only delivered the message once the hair had grown back!

The **Romans** also used secret messages – the powerful politician and general Julius Caesar even had one named after him! The Caesar shift is a **cipher** where one letter is swapped for another a certain number of places later in the alphabet.

Just before he was stabbed to death, Caesar's spies gave him a list of the people plotting to murder him – but he didn't read it!

Er, those knives look sharp!

MEDIEVAL MISSIONS

Caesar's spies couldn't save him, but espionage was alive and well long after the Romans were history. **Medieval** spies ranged from masters of disguise to deadly assassins.

Mythical minstrels?

Tum-tee-tum. Carry on, I'm just a minstrel!

This print shows Alfred spying on the Vikings. Just a legend? Maybe, but 'hiding in plain sight' is a key spy skill.

It's the 9th century and the **Vikings** are trying to invade England in search of land and treasure. A wandering **minstrel** strolls into the Viking camp playing his harp and singing. Hang on, that 'minstrel' might just be Alfred, the **Anglo-Saxon** king, spying on the enemy!

Three hundred years later, the English king Richard the Lionheart was being held prisoner in a secret castle. It's said he was rescued by a minstrel working as a spy. How did the spy know the king was there? He sang under the window and Richard joined in!

Assassins and Mongols

Some spies were involved in far more deadly missions. The 11th-century Persian leader Hassan-i-Sabbah founded a group of warriors who spied and were trained to murder specific **targets**. They came to be known as Assassins (the modern word for a hired killer).

Genghis Khan was the ruthless military leader of the **Mongols** at the beginning of the 13th century. Spies were central to his brutal conquest of other territories. For example, his invasion of the **Khwarezm Empire** depended not just on the espionage carried out by his own agents, but also on their ability to stop the enemy spying and feed them false information.

MUST BE ABLE TO:

ride a horse

Famed horseback riders, the Mongols had a quick and efficient communication system. They spaced out stations with fresh horses and food across the **empire**. Using a relay system of rapid riders, spies could pass messages over vast distances in a short time.

Mongol messengers could travel 200–300 km a day. This modern rider is dressed like a medieval Mongol soldier.

NINJA!

Who were the most legendary medieval spies? The ninja of Japan! People believed they could walk on water, transform into animals and even fly ...

Supernatural spies?

In the 15th century, Japan had an emperor but the real rulers were the *daimyo*. These powerful lords from different regions fought each other for control of land and power. They hired the ninja to get information on each other's land and buildings, or to steal secrets. Ninja were so fantastic at sneaking into places and escaping unseen, people believed they could make themselves invisible.

Ninja would usually dress in dark blue to move around under cover of night.

HAVE YOU GOT WHAT IT TAKES?
SHINOBI OR KUNOICHI

TOP SKILL: Dead good at disguise

Shinobi (male ninja) and *kunoichi* (female ninja) were experts in disguise. Men might dress as monks, musicians or soldiers; women as dancers or housekeepers. This allowed them to blend in and get close to enemies.

Dancer disguise

Monk disguise

Ninja tools included crowbars and folding saws for breaking into buildings, hooks and ropes for scaling walls, and a listening device shaped like a cone that allowed **eavesdropping** on quiet conversations. Wooden 'shoes' may have helped ninja cross castle **moats** or swamps without sinking, making it appear they could walk on water. It's even possible they made a 'hang-glider' by stringing cloth between two poles, allowing them to 'fly' for short distances.

A ninja? Who, me?

MUST BE ABLE TO:

use climbing claws

Ninja used metal claws like these to help them climb. When people saw the tracks the claws left behind, they believed the ninja had transformed into a cat or bear!

ELIZABETHAN ESPIONAGE

When Elizabeth I was queen of England (1558–1603), Sir Francis Walsingham and his spy network helped protect her life and keep her on the throne.

Spot the plot

Religion was very important in **Tudor** times (1485–1603). England started the Tudor period as Catholic, became Protestant during Henry VIII's reign, changed back to Catholic during the reign of his daughter Mary I and then back to Protestant during Elizabeth's reign. Confused? So were the English!

Some people wanted the Catholic Mary Queen of Scots (Elizabeth's cousin) on the throne instead. In 1586 Mary sent coded letters to her supporters, but they were intercepted and deciphered by Walsingham with deadly consequences ...

SUPER 🦁 SPYMASTER

NAME: Sir Francis Walsingham

NATIONALITY: English

AKA: Elizabeth I's top spy

ACHIEVEMENTS: He kept spies in England and abroad to track plots against the queen. When he uncovered Mary Queen of Scots' plot to take the throne, Elizabeth ordered Mary's execution in 1587.

HE SAID WHAT?

'See and keep silent.'

Walsingham's spies cracked plotters' codes and uncovered messages written in invisible ink.

Armada ahoy!

Walsingham's other worry was Spain. In 1588, the (Catholic) Spanish king Philip II sent the Armada — a fleet of over 100 ships — to invade England and overthrow Elizabeth. Thanks to Walsingham's many foreign spies, he knew the enemy's plans in advance, which helped to defeat the Spanish.

MUST BE ABLE TO:

write with invisible ink

Just pop to the shops for this Elizabethan essential. Secret notes written in lemon juice or milk are invisible until warmed. Don't forget to write a 'real' message in ordinary ink between the invisible lines so your note doesn't raise suspicion!

This painting shows the scale of Philip's so-called 'Invincible Armada'. He just didn't realise the English knew it was coming …

Philip II
(Mary I's husband)

Mary I
(Elizabeth's elder sister)

Henry VIII
(Mary and Elizabeth's father)

Elizabeth I

WASHINGTON'S SPIES

About 200 years after Walsingham was the top Tudor in English intelligence, 13 **colonies** in North America were fighting to escape British rule in the American War of Independence (1775–83).

SUPER SPYMASTER

NAME: George Washington

NATIONALITY: American

AKA: 'The father of the nation'

ACHIEVEMENTS: A military man who was a master of espionage, Washington used spies to uncover British secrets, and tricks to spread false information.

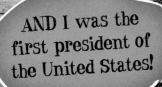

AND I was the first president of the United States!

Double crossing

John Honeyman, a British soldier, had been imprisoned by the Americans. He escaped and ran to tell the British how weak the opposition were. Except Harrison was a double agent working for Washington, and the 'weak' opposition soon beat the British army that had been fed the false information.

14

The Culper Ring

Washington also set up a **spy ring** to gather information about the movement, fortifications and tactics of British troops. The Culper Ring passed secret messages and used codenames to keep their identities hidden.

All spies know that espionage is a high-risk job and being discovered can be a matter of life and death. The Culper Ring were never caught, but others were not so lucky.

SECRET 🔱 SPY

NAME: Nathan Hale

NATIONALITY: American

AKA: Courageous captain

ACHIEVEMENTS: Remembered for his bravery and **patriotism**, Hale went behind enemy lines to spy on the British but was caught and hanged.

HE SAID WHAT?

'I only regret that I have but one life to lose for my country.'

Nathan Hale was just 21 when he was executed as a spy.

This statue of Nathan Hale stands at the headquarters of the CIA, the intelligence **agency** of the USA.

SPIES, LIES AND DISGUISE

Some of history's most amazing agents have been female — perhaps because people just didn't believe women could be spies. Big mistake! During the American Civil War (1861–5), women spied for both sides.

North v South

The American Civil War was fought between the country's Northern and Southern states. One of the main reasons was slavery, which was outlawed in the North but still legal in the South. Many slaves — wanting their freedom — supported the Northern army.

MUST BE ABLE TO:

send secret signals

The Dabneys were former slaves. Mrs Dabney was a laundress for Southern officers; Mr Dabney cooked in the Northern camp. Mrs Dabney sent her husband coded messages about the Southern army's movements — by the way she hung out the washing!

I freed 700 slaves in one raid!

SECRET 🛡 SPY

NAME: Harriet Tubman

NATIONALITY: American

SPYING FOR: the North

ACHIEVEMENTS: Tubman was born into slavery in Maryland. Before the war, she risked her life smuggling many slaves to freedom. She supported the North by carrying out reconnaissance and organising spy networks.

SECRET SPY

NAME: Belle Boyd

NATIONALITY: American

SPYING FOR: the South

ACHIEVEMENTS: Born in Virginia, Boyd worked as a Southern spy from the age of 17. Later she disguised herself as a boy and rode many kilometres on horseback to deliver information. Arrested a number of times, she became quite a celebrity.

> Bullets whistled past my ears on a battlefield!

SECRET SPY

NAME: Elizabeth van Lew

NATIONALITY: American

SPYING FOR: the North

ACHIEVEMENTS: Although a Southerner, van Lew was strongly against slavery and so spied for the North. Rather than use a disguise, she pretended to be mad – no one suspected 'Crazy Bet' of being a spy!

SECRET SPY

NAME: Sarah Emma Edmonds

NATIONALITY: Canadian

SPYING FOR: the North

ACHIEVEMENTS: Disguised as a man, Edmonds fought in the Northern army. Although there are no official records, she probably worked as a spy too, using different **aliases** including a white Irish woman called 'Bridget' and a black man called 'Cuff'.

THE FIRST WORLD WAR

Millions of people were caught up in the First World War (1914–18), so many lives were dependent on good spy work. Spying during the war involved **sabotage**, secret messages and surveillance.

Global conflict

The First World War was fought between two main groups of countries – Britain, France and Russia (and later the USA) on one side, and Germany, Austria–Hungary, the **Ottoman Empire** and Bulgaria on the other. Because some of these countries had empires, spies were active all around the world. Advances in technology were also important: messages sent by the relatively new telephone or radio had to avoid interception and decoding, and photography was used to gather all kinds of evidence.

Mata Hari was supposedly convicted after invisible ink was found in her make-up bag.

SECRET SPY

NAME: Margaretha Zelle

NATIONALITY: Dutch

AKA: Mata Hari

ACHIEVEMENTS: A dancer and celebrity, she had relationships with officers and politicians – both French and German. Although she claimed to be working for the French, she was arrested and executed as a German spy.

Reconnaissance aircraft like this British BE2 carried cameras to spy on German forces.

SECRET SPY

NAME: T E Lawrence

NATIONALITY: British

AKA: Lawrence of Arabia

ACHIEVEMENTS: The British were fighting the Ottoman Empire in the deserts of the Middle East. Lawrence worked with the local Bedouin tribes to use sabotage and raiding tactics against the enemy.

Peter O'Toole played Lawrence of Arabia in a famous film about his life.

MUST BE ABLE TO:

employ animal agents

Pigeons have been sent on spying missions since early times. Due to their 'homing instinct' and ability to fly quickly in all conditions, they were used to transport messages in both world wars.

SECRET SPY

NAME: Sidney Reilly

NATIONALITY: Russian

AKA: 'Ace of Spies'

ACHIEVEMENTS: The ultimate spy, his life is surrounded by mystery. It's thought he spied for four different countries, including Britain during the First World War. Pretending to be a German soldier, he sent information to England via carrier pigeon.

THE SECOND WORLD WAR

The Second World War (1939–45) was fought between the Allies (including Britain, France, the **Soviet Union** and the USA) and the Axis powers (Germany, Italy and Japan). Soldiers battled on the front lines, but thousands of secret agents also fought in the shadows.

Propaganda posters like this reminded people that enemy spies could be anywhere.

Keep mum she's not so dumb!

CARELESS TALK COSTS LIVES

HAVE YOU GOT WHAT IT TAKES?
ALLIES AGENT **

TOP SKILL: Level-headed linguist

If you knew an area and its language well, could think on your feet and hold your nerve, you could have been a Second World War spy. It didn't matter what your background was; agents included former circus acrobats, wrestlers, criminals – even an Indian princess.

Secret war

The Special Operations Executive (SOE) in Britain and the Office of Strategic Services (OSS) in the USA together had over 20,000 spies. Recruits were trained in sabotage, weapons and how to use codes and ciphers.

From 1940, British SOE agents parachuted at night into enemy territory to carry out reconnaissance and sabotage and help local people fight against the German occupation. They carried a new range of spy gadgets – lightweight hidden items such as knives hidden in pencils and fake books to hide documents.

SOE agents used 'suitcase radios' like this one to send and receive vital messages about agents' movements or supply drops.

SECRET SPY

NAME: Frederick 'Fritz' Duquesne

NATIONALITY: South African

AKA: Take your pick – he had at least 30 aliases

ACHIEVEMENTS: A spy for the Germans in both World Wars, he was imprisoned and escaped a number of times. He was finally caught when heading up the Duquesne spy ring in 1942.

The Duquesne spy ring was a German ring based in the USA. Its 33 members were exposed by a double agent and convicted.

THE 33 CONVICTED MEMBERS OF THE DUQUESNE SPY RING

CRACKING THE CODE

Spies have always used codes and ciphers. As technology advanced during the Second World War, so did the complexity of these codes – and the skills needed to crack them.

Unbreakable?

The Germans had a cipher machine called Enigma that they used to send coded messages, for example to direct submarine attacks. They believed it was completely unbreakable as Enigma had trillions of possible settings and the settings were changed daily.

Enigma **scrambled** messages by using rotors (wheels) to substitute the letters that were typed in.

Germany relied on Enigma-coded messages to guide its submarines towards enemy ships.

MUST BE ABLE TO:
solve crosswords

In 1942, a British newspaper ran a competition to solve a crossword in 12 minutes. The British military were looking for codebreakers. They invited the super-solvers for an interview!

The British used a team of maths, science, language and chess geniuses to try to crack Enigma. They worked from Bletchley Park in Buckinghamshire, a site so secret that nobody knew about the work carried out there until the 1970s. One of the leading codebreakers was the mathematician Alan Turing. Turing developed work carried out by the Polish before the war to design a machine called a 'bombe' that deciphered the code. Enigma was finally cracked – which some people say shortened the war by two years.

HAVE YOU GOT WHAT IT TAKES?
CODE TALKER

TOP SKILL: Knowledge of Navajo

The US army also used very effective codes during the war, in particular those based on native American languages such as Navajo. Navajo is a difficult language to learn and only a few non-Navajos spoke it. This meant the 'code talkers' did not need to scramble messages, but could send them quickly without worrying about them being deciphered.

This statue commemorates the Navajo code talkers. Their 'code' was never cracked.

AGENCIES AND AGENTS

Many countries have agencies to spy on each other. In wartime, they want to find out military strength and weakness. In peacetime, they might spy on more advanced countries to gain a technological advantage or on their own people to identify criminals or **terrorists**.

The name's Bond; James Bond!

Spy agencies

Some of the world's major spy agencies are:

- **MI6 (Military Intelligence, Section 6)**, the UK spy agency originally formed in 1909

- **the CIA (Central Intelligence Agency)** in the USA, formed in 1947

- **ISI (Inter-Service Intelligence)** in Pakistan, believed to have the largest number of agents in the world, formed in 1948

- **the FSB (Federal Security Services)** in Russia was formed in 1995 and replaced former spy agencies the NKVD and the KGB.

The fictional character James Bond works for MI6. Bond's creator, Ian Fleming, was also a real-life spy.

BMT 216A

HAVE YOU GOT WHAT IT TAKES?

** FIELD AGENT **

PERSONALITY PROFILE:
Outdoor type

Field agents are spies that work for a spy agency, but outside the agency building – in 'the field'. They might have to break into buildings, hide bugs or steal top-secret documents.

The Minox was the standard-issue camera for spies from the 1950s to the 1980s. Bond even used one in the film *You Only Live Twice.*

Tools of the trade

Bond is always being given gadgets, such as exploding watches and mobile phones with image identification. Real-life spies also use special tools, such as concealed weapons, bugs and cameras.

Guns have been hidden in gloves, pens and lipstick tubes. During the Cold War (see pages 26–27) spies used cameras disguised as coat buttons or watches. Modern digital cameras can be miniscule: the PI-Camcorder Tiny Tek can fit inside a chewing-gum packet.

MUST BE ABLE TO:

work with bugs

A bug is a tiny microphone that can be hidden almost anywhere. A spy might hide a bug in a light fitting, behind a picture or as part of a watch or pen, and then listen in to conversations from a nearby vehicle or next-door room.

THE COLD WAR

The USA and the Soviet Union had been allies in the Second World War. But after the war, these two **superpowers** were involved in the Cold War (1946–91). It was called 'cold' because the two countries did not fight directly; this time spies were the soldiers.

The Soviet Union used these giant planes to spy on the Americans.

Hunting for moles

A mole is a spy who is recruited by an agency, 'planted' in an enemy organisation and who stays there – maybe for years – passing bits and pieces of information back to their real bosses at the agency.

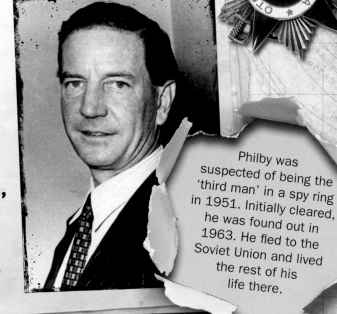

SECRET ♔ SPY

NAME: Kim Philby

NATIONALITY: British

AKA: The Third Man

ACHIEVEMENTS: A member of the 'Cambridge Five' spy ring, Philby worked for SOE and MI6 during the Second World War. In fact he was a double agent who had been recruited by the Soviet Union years earlier.

Philby was suspected of being the 'third man' in a spy ring in 1951. Initially cleared, he was found out in 1963. He fled to the Soviet Union and lived the rest of his life there.

HAVE YOU GOT WHAT IT TAKES?

**** MOLE ****

TOP SKILL: Living 'underground'

Can you imagine living your life pretending to be someone else? This is what moles have to do. A sleeper is a mole that might wait for years before undertaking a mission – sleepers often need that time to work their way up and access top-level information.

The testing of nuclear weapons like this US blast in 1951 only served to increase tension in the Cold War.

There were many moles in the Cold War they were often trying to find out what kind of **nuclear weapons** the other side had. Klaus Fuchs was a German–born British scientist who worked on the first US nuclear bombs. Julius and Ethel Rosenberg were US citizens who were also **communists**. Fuchs and the Rosenbergs passed information about US nuclear weapons to the Soviet Union.

The Rosenbergs were executed in 1953 after being exposed as spies.

MODERN SPIES

The world of espionage is always changing. Governments use technology to help fight terrorism, but that technology means there is an increasing threat from **cyber** spies.

Cyber spies and whistleblowers

One of the main tasks for modern spies is helping to fight terrorism. Intelligence agencies use all the resources they can to keep track of terrorist groups and anticipate attacks. Many people think cyber warfare – using computers to disable defence systems or cut power supplies – is the next big threat.

People who break into computer systems are called hackers. Not all hackers are bad: white-hat hackers are often hired to test a computer system's security. 'Grey hats' break in and then alert the organisation that they've done it. However, 'black hats' are criminals who hack in to steal data, such as bank details.

MUST BE ABLE TO:

get to grips with biometrics

People have used fingerprints as a way to identify someone for hundreds of years. Now there are even more accurate ways to identify someone: facial and voice recognition, iris (eye) scanning and checking your DNA, which is unique to you. That big hat and fake beard just won't cut it anymore!

Spying has always been shrouded in secrecy, but whistleblowers are people who think that the public deserve to know about different groups' secret activities. WikiLeaks is a whistleblowing website set up by Australian Julian Assange that posts **classified** information for anyone to see.

Whistleblower Edward Snowden, a former CIA worker, leaked secret information about global surveillance.

HAVE YOU GOT WHAT IT TAKES?

*** FUTURE SPY ***

TOP SKILL: Quick thinking, cool in a crisis, gutsy, creative … there are lots!

Despite fast-changing technology, there are still agents in the field and it's likely that human spies will always be needed. So how do you get the job? Some people are asked to join, but you can also just apply. Strange as it may seem, spy agencies advertise – just like any other company!

The Internet age makes cyber attacks possible, but it also means intelligence can be gathered more easily and information spread instantly.

GLOSSARY

BCE – the letters BCE stand for 'before common era'. They refer to dates before the year CE 1.

CE – the letters CE stand for 'common era'. They refer to dates after the year CE 1.

agency – an organisation

alias – an assumed identity

Anglo-Saxon – a group of people who lived in Britain from about 450 to 1066

cipher – a code that substitutes letters for others, for example A becomes D, B becomes E and so on

city-state – in ancient Greece, an independent area based around a city or an island

classified – only available to authorised people

colony – an area under the control of another country

communist – someone who believes all property should be shared

corrupt – willing to act dishonestly, often in return for money

cyber – to do with computers

double agent – a spy who pretends to work for someone while really working for their enemy

eavesdrop – listen secretly

empire – a group of countries ruled over by one country

espionage – spying

Khwarezm Empire – a medieval empire that covered parts of modern Iran, Uzbekistan and Turkmenistan

medieval – relating to the period 500–1500 in European history

minstrel – a singer or musician

moat – a water-filled ditch surrounding a castle

nuclear weapon – a weapon of mass destruction powered by energy from atoms

patriotism – love for your country

propaganda – information that tries to make people think a certain way

reconnaissance – exploring an area to gather (usually military) information

sabotage – damaging or destroying something on purpose

scramble – make a message unable to be understood (unless deciphered)

Soviet Union – a former country (1922–91) made up of 15 states (see map below)

spy ring – a group of spies working together

superpower – a very powerful country

target – a person, object or place selected for investigation or attack

terrorist – someone who uses violence and fear for political reasons

Tudor – an English royal family who reigned from 1485 to 1603

Soviet Union

ANCIENT CIVILISATIONS

GREEKS
(750–30 BCE) – an advanced Mediterranean civilisation that studied science, maths and medicine.

PERSIANS
(c. 550–330 BCE) – the first Persian empire was founded by Cyrus the Great (reigned 559–530 BCE) and eventually conquered by Alexander the Great.

VIKINGS
(CE 700–1100)
– a group of people originally from Scandinavia that conquered land across northern Europe and the north Atlantic, creating a Viking empire.

Vikings
Mongols
Greeks
Persians
Ottoman Empire
Roman Empire

MONGOLS
(CE 1206–1335)
– an empire that stretched from Central Europe to Japan, which was created by Genghis Khan.

ROMANS
(753 BCE–CE 476)
– a highly developed civilisation that built a vast empire. The Roman Empire was at its greatest extent around CE 117.

OTTOMAN EMPIRE
(CE 1299–1923)
– an empire based around Turkey that was at its height during the reign of Suleiman the Magnificent (1494–1566). It collapsed after the First World War.

INDEX

Further information

www.spymuseum.org/education-programs/kids-families/kidspy-zone/

Play games, learn to talk like a spy and even transform into a Bond villain at the International Spy Museum website.

www.bbc.co.uk/history/british/tudors/launch_gms_spying.shtml

Play the Elizabethan Spying Game to crack the code that caught Mary Queen of Scots.

Every effort has been made by the Publishers to ensure that the websites in this book are suitable for children, that they are of the highest educational value, and that they contain no inappropriate or offensive material. However, because of the nature of the Internet, it is impossible to guarantee that the contents of these sites will not be altered. We strongly advise that Internet access is supervised by a responsible adult.